A Beginners Guide to Roth IRAs and 401(k)-Type Plans

Also Available by Keith Dorney

**Becoming Financially Independent**
book series

Best Debt Elimination Plan _Debt Management Strategies that Get You Out of Debt Quickly and Economically_

A Beginners Guide to Roth IRAs and 401(k)-Type Plans: _Contribution, Conversion, and Withdrawal Strategies for Building Tax-Free Wealth_

DIY Stock and Securities Investing: _Investment Strategies for Building Wealth and Attaining Financial Independence_

Maximize Your Earnings with a Health Savings Account: _Learn how a Health Savings Account can save you money. Take advantage of 4 tax breaks and seriously consider investing some of those contributions._

A Beginners Guide to Roth IRAs and 401(k)-Type Plans

Contribution, Conversion, and Withdrawal Strategies for Building Tax-Free Wealth

Keith Dorney CFP® MA

https://keithdorney.com

Disclaimer:

The information contained within this book is not and should not be construed as financial or investment advice: Advice can only be given once an advisor has a deeper understanding of an individual's complete financial situation. The information in this book should be considered of a general educational nature, not financial or investment advice.

This book will educate you with what is hoped to be correct and up-to-date information, but no warranty or promise is made that everything is 100% accurate.

This book is published as a print-on-demand book for a reason: I update it every year. I take pride in providing only the most up-to-date information in easy-to-understand language.

This work was originally published with the title *Best Roth! A Beginner's Guide to Roth IRAs, Employer Roth Options, Conversions, and Withdrawals* by Keith Dorney.

Table of Contents

For a **Detailed Table of Contents**, see **page 121**

Table of Contents

Your Best Roth

Finding your best Roth—accounts that match your investment objectives and have low fees—can be confusing.

If you're a seasoned investor, your best Roth might be part of a diversified portfolio of both Roth and pre-tax (traditional) investments, including IRAs, company-sponsored plans, and a regular taxable account.

On the other hand, if you're just starting, your best Roth could be a single investment in your employer's plan or a Roth IRA.

So, the best Roth for one investor may not be the best for another.

No matter your situation, I recommend investing in tax-advantaged accounts like Roth vehicles before investing in a regular taxable account. For goals like financial independence, retirement, and other longer-term goals, it's a no-brainer: You'll earn a higher after-tax rate of return because of the tax advantages!

I'll help you incorporate your employer's plan (if any) and IRA(s) into your financial plan. If you don't have a financial plan, I'll help you get started coming up with a good one (*Roth Investments and Your Financial Plan, page 105*).

Then there are the IRS rules and interpretations governing Roth IRAs and company-sponsored plans. They can be complicated. I'll explain them in easy-to-understand language, and enlighten you on some advantageous interpretations of which you may not be aware:

- You may be able to contribute to a Roth IRA even if you're over the income limits, and potentially do so well above the maximum yearly contribution limit. [*The 'Ole Roth IRA Switcheroo, page 41*]
- If you have a retirement plan at work, like a 401(k), 403(b), or 457 plan, it's still smart to fund a Roth IRA in addition to your payroll deductions and match (if any), even if your employer offers a Roth option. [*Roth IRA versus 401(k)-Type Plans, page 35*]
- If you're married and have a non-working spouse, chances are you can open a Roth IRA for your spouse even though he or she has no earned income. [*Spousal Roth IRA, page 71*]
- If one has earned income, regardless of age, you are eligible to contribute to a Roth IRA. That includes your kids. They'll thank you

profusely later for urging them to start their tax-free earnings so early. [*Minor Roth IRA and Saver's Credit, page 75*]

- I've found a lot of folks get confused as to when they can take money out of their Roth IRAs tax-free. It's no wonder—the IRS ordering rules can be hard to fathom. A Roth IRA remains one of the few retirement accounts where money can be tapped penalty and tax-free before age 59 1/2. This is especially important to those of you who want to achieve financial independence earlier than later. [*IRS Ordering Rules, page 63*]

- If you're hoping to pass money along to the next generation, a Roth investment shines like no other. No required minimum distributions allow you to not only actively invest in your Roth until the day you die but pass it along tax-free to your beneficiaries. [*Designating Your Roth IRA Beneficiary, page 83*]

- You can use the funds in your Roth IRA for goals other than financial independence and retirement. Rules allow penalty-free withdrawals for college and a "first-time" home purchase, and over the years your Roth IRA can act as a backup emergency reserve fund. [*Using a Roth IRA for Other Financial Goals, page 95*]

- I want you to utilize Roth IRAs and employer-sponsored Roth options to help you achieve your longer-term goals, but are you maximizing your earnings and at the same time minimizing your risks? [*Roth Investments and Your Financial Plan, page 105*]

Where Can I Make My Roth Contributions?

You have many choices when deciding where to invest Roth contributions. If your employer's plan offers a Roth option, you can make Roth and/or traditional contributions to the same employer-sponsored plan, up to the contribution limits.

Many employers don't offer a retirement savings option, or they offer a plan but haven't amended it to allow Roth contributions. That leaves you with a Roth IRA as your only option.

Most financial institutions that offer investments are also authorized Roth IRA custodians. That means banks, credit unions, brokerage houses, insurance companies, mutual fund companies, discount brokers, and more all offer Roth IRAs.

Most products that financial institutions offer are fair game for investment in your Roth IRA, but you must keep them "contained." For example, you might have a traditional IRA account, a Roth IRA account, as well as a regular taxable account with the same financial institution: Your Roth IRA can't be commingled with those other accounts, or your tax-free earnings advantage will be lost.

Multitude of Investments

That means you can invest in individual securities like stocks and bonds, index or actively managed mutual funds, exchange-traded funds, commodities like gold, silver, pork bellies, or cattle futures, even some derivatives and foreign currency trading are possible.

Then there are the *Self-Directed Roth IRAs (page 89)* where investing in real estate, private businesses, precious metals, and private loans may be possible.

Don't be intimidated. Whatever your knowledge and skill level as an investor, I'll help you get the most out of your tax-advantaged accounts. *A Beginners Guide to Roth IRAs and 401(k)-Type Plans* is packed with up-to-date information for both novice and seasoned investors.

Tax-free Earning on Tax-free Earnings

Tax-free earnings trump taxable earnings, especially if you expect to double, triple, or quintuple your money, and it sure beats being "held hostage" by Uncle Sam. That's one of the big advantages Roth investments have over pre-tax/traditional savings vehicles, and why I believe they should be in everyone's investing lineup.

Who knows what ordinary income tax rates are going to be when you finally take that money out of those traditional retirement savings vehicles? Ordinary income tax rates are subject to change, and if I had to guess if taxes are going to be higher or lower when you decide to tap that money, I'd have to guess higher. Wouldn't you?

Unlike traditional savings vehicles, where you're not sure how much Uncle Sam is going to let you keep, Roth contributions and earnings have a federal tax tab of exactly 0% upon qualified withdrawals: You paid the tax tab on the contribution in the year you made it, and earnings (if deemed qualified) can be withdrawn tax-free.

As far as state tax goes, there is a real mishmash of rules out there, and why this book addresses federal taxation only. Visit the IRS website *http://www.irs.gov/Businesses/Small-Businesses-&-*

Self-Employed/State-Links-1 to get more information on how your state deals with Roth distributions.

Roth Information at Your Fingertips

I've organized things so you can find the information you need quickly and easily.

In addition to the regular Table of Contents at the front of the book, there is a more detailed one at the back starting on page 121 if you're looking for a particular Roth subject.

Or, read the chapters sequentially. Each subject builds on the preceding ones, but each chapter is its own entity, so feel free to jump around (if you haven't already). *I update this book every year and whenever necessary, so you're assured of getting all the latest and up-to-date Roth information.*

Contribution Limits

The following IRA contribution limits are the maximum allowed. Whether you're making all Roth contributions or all traditional contributions, or you're making both Roth and traditional IRA contributions, your combined contributions for the year cannot exceed these thresholds:

IRA Contribution Limits 2026

IRA Max Contribution Age 49 and Younger 2026	
Regular Contribution	$7,500

If you're age 50 or older there is an extra catch-up contribution available:

IRA Max Contributions Age 50 and Older 2026	
Regular Contribution	+7,500
Catch-Up Contribution	+1,100
	=$8,600

You've got to keep your IRA contributions separated: Pre-tax contributions go in your traditional IRA, and Roth contributions go into your Roth IRA. Both the IRA contribution limit and the catch-up are now indexed for inflation.

Roth and traditional contributions to your employer's 401(k)-type plan, on the other hand, *are* made to the same account and subject to the following limitations:

401(k)-type Plan Contribution Limits 2026

401(k) Max Contribution Age 49 and Younger 2026	
Regular Contribution	**$24,500**

401(k) Max Contributions Age 50 and Older 2026	
Regular Contribution	+24,500
Catch-Up Contribution	+8,000
	=$32,500

401(k) Max Contributions Ages 60-63 for 2026	
Regular Contribution	+24,500
Enhanced Catch-Up Contribution	+11,250
	=$35,750

2026 employee catch-up contributions are limited to Roth-only designated contributions if their prior year's wages are greater than $150,000. This rule pertains to catch-up contributions only.

Throughout the text, I refer to these employer-sponsored plans as 401(k)-type plans because from the employee's perspective, 401(k)s, 403(b)s, 457, 401(a), and the government-sponsored TSP plan all have similar characteristics.

Your employer may offer a different plan with different maximums. Employers are not obligated to offer all the provisions covered here, so consult your employer's employee benefits website.

Most contribution maximums, income limits, and other dollar limitations are pegged to inflation. They'll be outdated next year. Be sure to stay informed of those and other changes in the years to come.

Don't confuse the amount you can contribute with the amount you can convert. There are no limits to the amount you can convert to a Roth IRA, whether that conversion comes from a company-sponsored retirement plan, a traditional IRA, or both. See the 'Ole Roth IRA Switcheroo (page 41) and Roth Conversions and Rollovers (page 53) chapters for details.

Contribute On or Before the Deadline

With most employer-sponsored plans, contributions must be made within the calendar year through payroll deductions.

With IRAs, you have until April 15th following the end of the calendar year to contribute. For 2026 contributions, you have until April 15th, 2027, to make a 2026 contribution. These due dates are *not* extended if you file for a tax extension.

If you expect a tax refund, there are few better places to stash that extra cash than a Roth IRA. If you're contributing between January 1st and April 15th for the previous calendar year, be sure it's clear to your IRA trustee that the contribution is for the *previous* year. (During that time, you're able to contribute for the previous year or the current year; if you choose the current year by mistake, you'll lose out on a year's contribution option.)

Above are the maximum Roth contribution limits: Don't think you have to contribute the full amount. Most 401(k)-type plans have no minimum contribution amount. Many Roth IRA accounts allow contributions as little as $50.

When is Your Birthday?

Even if you turn 50 on December 31st, you still qualify to make the higher of the two contribution limits. It's the same for the new 60-63 enhanced catch-up provision. For example, say you turn 50 on December 31, 2026. You're still eligible to contribute $32,500 to a 401(k)-type plan, and $8,600 to a Roth IRA for the calendar year 2026.

Traditional versus Roth

Before opening and funding a Roth investment, make sure you're making the right type of contribution. A Roth contribution is not the only tax-advantaged investment in town: Traditional contributions have their own set of advantages. It's not always easy to decide.

Whether you're an employee and have both a traditional (pre-tax) and Roth option in your company's 401(k)-type plan, or you have no employer-sponsored option and you contribute to IRAs instead, you're faced with a similar dilemma:

What type of contributions should I be making — traditional or Roth?

Traditional earnings accrue tax-deferred, not tax-free like a Roth, but earn the taxpayer a tax deduction in the year of the contribution. Tax on yearly contributions is also deferred; however, 100% of all distributions (contributions plus earnings) will be taxed at ordinary income tax rates upon withdrawal.

Whether you're making traditional contributions to a 401(k)-type plan or to a traditional IRA, it works the same way.

Roth earnings accrue tax-free, not tax-deferred like traditional pre-tax contributions. Since earnings accrue tax-free, and tax has already been levied on the contribution in the year it was made, 100% of all distributions (contributions + earnings) are tax-free upon qualified withdrawal.

Whether you're making Roth contributions to a 401(k)-type plan or to a Roth IRA, it works the same way.

Two Separate Accounts?

Many savers maintain both a Roth IRA and a traditional IRA, often at the same financial institution, making contributions to one or a combination of the two in any given tax year.

Traditional and Roth IRA contributions must be made to separate accounts: Traditional and Roth monies cannot be commingled in the Individual Retirement Account world. Contributions can be made to one or both accounts in any given calendar year, but the total combination contributed cannot exceed the contribution limit for the calendar year.

This can be confusing to some employees because with most 401(k)-type plans traditional and Roth contributions *can* be made to the same account.

Don't worry—your employer keeps track of earnings attributed to each type of contribution, so you'll know definitively what "flavor" (taxable or tax-free) your money is when you withdraw it.

You can change the status of your retirement money from traditional to Roth via a Roth IRA conversion; however, tax must be paid—at ordinary income tax rates—on the entire amount converted in the year the conversion takes place. Money cannot be converted from Roth to traditional.

Pay Taxes Now or Later

A taxpayer benefits more from traditional contributions in the year the contribution is made. Everything else being equal, making a traditional contribution versus a Roth contribution will generate higher net income in the year of the contribution because of tax savings. The higher your tax bracket the bigger the savings.

If you had answers to the following questions, you'd be able to figure more accurately which type of contribution benefits you more. Unfortunately, there are many unknowns, and the ambiguity is greater the younger you are:

- How much tax will be assessed when I withdraw my traditional (pre-tax) contributions and earnings?
- What will my rate of return be?
- How long will I live?
- How much money will be withdrawn and when?
- What will my yearly budget be in retirement?
- What year will I start taking withdrawals from my Roth IRA?

Of course, you can make educated guesses as to the answers to these questions, but you won't know for sure. That's what makes deciding so difficult.

The prospect of higher tax rates is especially troubling. Every time Uncle Sam raises ordinary income tax rates, that means less money for retirement as far as your traditional contributions and earnings go.

Part of the utility of traditional contributions is the prospect of being in a lower tax bracket when you withdraw funds than you were when you contributed years earlier. That assumption could be incorrect if ordinary income tax rates drift higher.

If you're unsure how our tax system works, the following is a quick refresher.

Ordinary Income Tax Rates

Ordinary income is taxed at ordinary income tax rates. Ordinary income is often referred to as W-2 income because your employer reports your income to both you and the IRS on that form. If you're an employee, more than likely this represents most of your income.

Salary, wages, tips, bonuses, commissions, as well as most other compensation paid by your employer are all considered ordinary income. If your employer offers restricted stock units, stock options, or an ESPP plan, all or part of those acquisitions and liquidations will be added to your ordinary income tax tab as well.

If you work as an independent contractor rather than an employee, income is reported on Form 1099 and is also considered ordinary income.

Social Security payments (up to 85%) are treated as ordinary income on your tax return, as well as most pension payments and non-Roth withdrawals from employer-sponsored retirement plans.

From this income, certain deductions are allowed:

- Adjustments to Income
- The Standard Deduction or Itemized Deductions (whichever is higher)

Keep in mind most of these deductions have income limits, meaning if you make too much money, your deduction may be reduced or eliminated.

After subtracting out these deductions from our ordinary income, we arrive at our taxable income. It's our taxable income we take to the tax tables to compute the amount of tax we owe for the year.

Currently, income tax rates start at 10%. Regardless of the amount of your taxable income or your filing method, that first hunk of money gets taxed at 10%.

There are 4 different ways to file your taxes. The most common are *single* and *married filing jointly*, but you can also file as *head of household* or *married filing separately* (if you qualify). Each filing method has its own income thresholds for the seven different tax brackets.

Depending on the size of your taxable income, you progress from 10% to 12%, then 22%, 24%, 32%, 35% and finally 37%.

It's these taxable income thresholds, as well as the tax rates themselves, that can change over time. Most recently, our government changed rates in 2013 and again in 2018. If history repeats itself, that means there will be changes between now and when you retire.

If I had to guess if tax rates would be higher or lower by the time I'm ready to make pre-tax withdrawals, I'd have to go with higher. Wouldn't you?

Required Minimum Distributions

Required minimum distributions, or RMDs, affect traditional IRAs and 401(k)-type plans but not Roth IRAs. It's all about Uncle Sam wanting his tax money.

The Secure Act 2.0 was passed by Congress and signed into law at the end of 2022. Its provisions increased the starting age for RMDs to 73 for 2023, rising incrementally to a starting age of 75 in 2033.

The start of RMDs forces you to take money out of your traditional IRAs, most employer-sponsored plans, and all other pre-tax accounts, whether you want to or not. That includes pre-tax contributions, most company matches, and associated earnings from 401(k)-type plans too.

If you decide not to comply, a 25% penalty is levied on the amount you were supposed to take out (down from a 50% penalty previously).

Another provision of Secure 2.0 is employees are now able to keep Roth funds in their employer-sponsored plan past their RMD age. Previously, employees had to roll Roth funds to a Roth IRA to avoid RMDs. That silly antiquated rule is no more.

The amount you must take out is based on the average life span of your age group at the time you turn your RMD age. That means if you live longer than the average person, all your pre-tax money will be taxed and out of your retirement accounts.

Roth IRAs and Roth money in 401(k)-type plans have no RMDs, which means you can invest and grow your investments tax-free for the latter years of your retirement. If you don't make it to the latter years of your retirement, your Roth beneficiaries inherit the tax-free cash rather than the taxable cash.

Should I Make Roth or Traditional Contributions?

That leaves the traditional versus Roth contribution quandary: If I can contribute to both, what type of contribution should I make? The answer may be all Roth contributions, all traditional contributions, or a combination of the two.

Estate planning objectives aside, it depends on your age, tax bracket, and income needs for the year.

Let's say you're twenty-one and just getting started in the workplace. You'll probably want to make all Roth contributions.

Unless you're a professional athlete or Hollywood movie star, you're paying tax in the lower tax brackets at this point. It just makes sense to get that tax liability over with while it's so low.

Plus, your time horizon for investment is extremely long (around 40 years), so lots and lots of tax-free earnings can be expected, making the choice a no brainer.

Contrarily, say you're in your fifties, at the top of your pay scale at work, have two kids in college, and plan on retiring soon. You'll probably want to make all traditional contributions.

That tax deduction is more valuable than ever now that you're paying tax in the higher brackets. Making a Roth contribution in lieu of a traditional one at this point costs you big bucks, which you may need to pay for your kids' tuition. Finally, because you're retiring soon, earnings will be limited, thus reducing the utility of tax-free earnings.

Dual Retirement Income is Best

Your choice may lie somewhere in between those two extremes. In some years it will be clear-cut which type of contribution to make, while in others it may be more muddled.

That's why the best solution is to have both traditional and Roth contributions working for you. That way you can have both a taxable and a non-taxable source of income in retirement, diversify the way you're saving, and protect against unforeseen tax rate increases.

Income Limits for Roth and Traditional IRAs

If you and/or your spouse are higher wage earners, you may not be able to make a direct contribution to a Roth IRA. If you and/or your spouse participate in an employer-sponsored retirement plan, there are also income limits governing deductible traditional IRA contributions.

But first, you must find your MAGI.

Finding Your MAGI

It's your MAGI that determines your options, which stands for Modified Adjusted Gross Income.

MAGI is your adjusted gross income with adjustments to account for foreign income, passive gains, and deductions like student loan interest, adoption expenses, and traditional IRA contributions.

Your Adjusted Gross Income from last year can be found at the bottom of the first page of your tax return.

Roth IRA Income Limits 2026

Roth IRA income limits apply whether you and/or your spouse participate in your employer's plan, or you don't—it doesn't matter. *The limits are the limits.*

Roth IRA Income Limits for 2026			
Filing Method	Max Allowed	Partial Allowed	None Allowed
Single, Married Filing Separately, Head of Household	MAGI less than $153,000	MAGI 153,000 - $168,000	MAGI greater than $168,000
Married Filing Jointly	MAGI less than $242,000	MAGI $242,000 - $252,000	MAGI greater than $252,000

Under the Limits

If you're under the income limits, you can make contributions directly to a Roth IRA as well as your 401(k)-type plan. If you're over the limits you can't contribute directly to a Roth IRA, but you could still contribute to your 401(k)-type plan.

Between the Thresholds

A "Partial contribution" means that if your MAGI is between those amounts, the maximum contribution amount is proportionally reduced from $7,500 (for the year 2026) to $0 as you approach the upper threshold.

If your employer (and your spouse's employer if you're married) doesn't offer a retirement savings option and you're over the Roth IRA income limits, you still can't contribute directly to a Roth IRA, but you could contribute to a traditional IRA.

Over the Limits

If your MAGI exceeds the limit for making a direct Roth IRA contribution, you may still be able to get money into one, but you have to get a bit creative. Those tricks are explained in *The 'Ole Roth IRA Switcheroo* chapter.

Traditional IRA Income Limits 2026

If your employer (and your spouse's employer if you're married) doesn't offer a retirement plan (many do not), these income limits for contributing to a traditional IRA do *not* apply, and you can make the maximum contribution to a traditional IRA regardless of your level of income.

However, if you and/or your spouse's employer(s) do offer a retirement plan like a 401(k)-type plan, the following *MAGI limits for traditional IRA contributions apply*:

You or Your Spouse are Covered by an Employer Retirement Plan (2026)			
You're Covered			
If you file as...	**No Deduction**	**Partial Deduction**	**Full Deduction**
Single or Head of Household	$91,000 or more	$81,000-$91,000	$81,000 or less
Married Filing Jointly	$149,00 or more	$129,000-149,000	129,000 or less
Married Filling Separate	$10,000 or more	Less than $10,000	n/a
Your Spouse is Covered			
If you file as...	**No Deduction**	**Partial Deduction**	**Full Deduction**
Married Filing Jointly	$246,000 or more	$236,000-$246,000	$236,000 or less
Married Filling Separate	$10,000 or more	Less than $10,000	n/a

Roth IRA versus 401(k)-Type Plan

It's best not to choose. If you can, contribute to **both** your company's plan and a Roth IRA every year for **these 4 reasons:**

Reason #1: Accessibility

You may think if you're offered a 401(k), 403(b), 457, 401(a) or similar type plan at work, especially if your employer offers a Roth contribution option, why bother with a Roth IRA? One big reason is accessibility. The money in your 401(k)-type plan is pretty much locked up until you turn age 59 1/2.

Yes, you can take a hardship withdrawal or borrow money from it, but the former comes with tax and a possible 10% early withdrawal penalty, while the latter wallops you with double taxation.

Contributions you made to your Roth IRA over the years are accessible at any time for any reason with no tax or penalty. I've found a lot of folks don't know this. (Maybe they're better off not knowing?)

You don't have to be age 59 1/2 or even have a good reason. Just don't withdraw more than the total of your past yearly contributions. This could come in handy in the event of an emergency, a big medical bill, or if you're a bit short coming up with the down payment for a house.

Example: Kat is 35 and has been making yearly $5,000 contributions to her Roth IRA for the last 5 years. Her current account balance is $35,000. Kat could withdraw $25,000 from her Roth IRA *tax and penalty free* to pay for a master's degree, help fund a house purchase, pay off high-interest credit card debt, or go on an expensive holiday.

The $10,000 in earnings, however, must stay in her account for a few more decades if she wants her withdrawals to be tax and penalty free.

Reason #2: Higher Contribution Limits and No Income Limits

The 401(k)-type plan contribution limit is much higher than IRA contribution limits. You can contribute over 3 times as much per year to a 401(k)-type plan versus an IRA.

If you're age 49 or younger, the 2026 contributions limits are $24,500 for a 401(k)-type plan versus $7,500 for an IRA, or $32,500 versus $8,600 if you're age 50 or older.

Roth IRAs have **MAGI limits**, but 401(k)-type plans do not. Unless your employer's plan is considered "top heavy" and you're labeled a highly compensated employee, you can contribute up to the maximum to your 401(k)-type plan no matter how high your income.

There is a way around those income limits for Roth IRAs if you're a higher wage earner. It's a little trick I call the *'Ole Roth IRA Switcheroo*.

Reason #3: No Required Minimum Distributions

When it comes to comparing 401(k)-type plans versus Roth IRAs, there is another reason why you need both: 401(k)s are subject to required minimum distributions (RMDs), while Roth IRAs are *not* subject to RMDs.

Only the pre-tax (traditional) portion of your 401(k)-type plan, including the contribution itself and any earnings, is subject to RMDs. Roth 401(k) contributions and earnings are *not* subject to RMDs or tax.

RMDs are all about Uncle Sam wanting his tax money. That means your 401(k)-type plan could be left high and dry come the latter years of your retirement, while your Roth IRA continues to rack up tax-free earnings until the day you die.

Reason #4: Take Advantage of Employer Contributions

Not all employers offer a match or non-elective contribution, but if they do, you must have your 401(k) plan up and running. Otherwise, that money your employer is trying to give you for your retirement will be lost forever.

Some employers offer a match but only allow you to make traditional or pre-tax contributions. If you'd rather make Roth contributions, contribute just enough to your company plan to get the full match, then stash the rest of those retirement dollars in your Roth IRA.

If you still want to contribute more than the Roth IRA contribution limits allow, increase your contribution percentage in your 401(k)-type vehicle in addition to maxing out your Roth IRA.

There are several reasons why you'd only want to make Roth IRA contributions and shun your company's 401(k) altogether. One reason is if your company offers no match, you prefer Roth contributions over traditional contributions, and you aren't planning on investing more than the

Roth IRA contribution limit. Another would be if your company offers no match and has lousy investment options.

401(k)-Type Plan or Roth IRA?

There's no need to decide. If you're lucky enough to be offered a retirement savings option at work, it most likely makes sense for you to invest in your employer's plan and a Roth IRA.

That way you'll have both taxable and non-taxable withdrawal options once you reach retirement, as well as more peace of mind if a financial emergency strikes. Think of it as diversifying the way you save.

The 'Ole Roth IRA Switcheroo

You may be able to enjoy tax-free earnings from a Roth IRA *even if you're over the MAGI income limits* for making Roth IRA contributions.

If your modified adjusted gross income is above the income limits, direct contributions to your Roth IRA are prohibited. Time for what I like to call the 'ole Roth IRA switcheroo. There are two types of switcheroos: The traditional IRA switcheroo and the 401(k)-type plan switcheroo.

Traditional IRA Switcheroo

This switcheroo involves first making a non-deductible after-tax contribution to a traditional IRA and then converting it to a Roth IRA.

Anyone, regardless of income, can make a non-deductible after-tax contribution to a traditional IRA, and anyone, regardless of income, can convert a traditional IRA to a Roth IRA, so no rules are being broken here.

This can be confusing. Aren't traditional IRA contributions supposed to be tax deductible? Yes, they are, but not if you or your spouse have a 401(k)-type plan and make too much money. If you do, income limits apply and, depending on your modified adjusted gross income (MAGI), a traditional IRA contribution may or may not be tax deductible.

Anyone, regardless of income, can make the non-deductible traditional IRA type of contribution, up to the IRA contribution limits. It can be made to either a new traditional IRA or an existing one.

As the name implies, there is no tax deduction on the contribution (like a Roth), but earnings accrue tax deferred, not tax-free like in a Roth IRA. That's why you're going to eventually convert those funds to a Roth IRA.

The traditional IRA switcheroo won't work if you already have pre-tax money in one or more traditional IRA-type accounts because of the IRS's pro-rata rule. You could have pre-tax funds in a traditional IRA that you rolled over from an old 401(k)-type plan, or from a time when you made deductible traditional IRA contributions.

Author's Note: I first named this little trick the 'ole Roth IRA switcheroo over a decade ago when teaching high-tech employees this maneuver, but for some reason the name never caught on. These days it's most referred to as a *back-door Roth IRA*.

Beware the Pro Rata Rule

If you already have a traditional IRA, SEP IRA, SIMPLE IRA, or other IRA-type account with pre-tax contributions, you may want to rethink this particular switcheroo strategy. The IRS's pro-rata rule states you must convert a proportional amount of pre-tax and post-tax amounts from all your accounts combined.

The IRS doesn't let you choose which flavor (pre-tax or post-tax) of contribution you are converting. You must convert a pro-rata portion of each. If all you have in your traditional IRA is that post-tax contribution, no tax will be owed on the contribution when you convert it, but tax will be owed on any accrued earnings from the time of the deposit until the conversion.

On the other hand, if you previously made deductible traditional IRA contributions or rolled over a 401(k), 403(b), 457 or other pre-tax employer-sponsored plan to a traditional IRA, those funds must be counted in the conversion ratio.

A conversion still could make sense, even if you must include a portion of your deductible contributions. Just make sure you have all the facts.

Traditional Switcheroo Example 1

Last year you rolled over $5,000 from your former employer's 401(k) into a traditional IRA. This year you want to do the 'ole Roth IRA switcheroo with a $5,000 non-deductible traditional IRA contribution because you're over the MAGI limit. 50% (5,000/10,000) of the $5,000 conversion, or $2,500, would be subject to ordinary income tax.

Traditional IRA Switcheroo Example 2

Last year you rolled over $195,000 from your former employer's 401(k) into your traditional IRA. This year you want to do the 'ole Roth IRA switcheroo with a $5,000 non-deductible traditional IRA contribution because you're over the MAGI limit. 97.5% (195/200) of the $5,000 conversion, or $4,875, would be subject to ordinary income tax.

Traditional IRA Switcheroo Example 3

You've never rolled over any money into a traditional IRA type vehicle, nor have you ever made contributions to one. You make a $5,000 non-deductible traditional IRA contribution because you're over the MAGI limits. Later, you convert that $5,000 to a Roth IRA. $0 tax is owed on the $5,000 conversion. You'll only pay tax on any earnings that may have accrued from the time of the contribution until you convert it. **All future earnings in your Roth IRA accrue tax-free!**

Employer Retirement Plan Switcheroo

If your employer allows what are known as non-Roth after-tax contributions to their 401(k)-type plan, you may have an even better opportunity. This option is especially delectable to big savers and/or higher wage earners who want to reach financial independence sooner than later. It lets you save in a tax-advantaged nature well beyond the yearly contribution limits.

For 2026, the contribution limit for defined contribution plans like 401(k)-type plans is $24,500 if you're age 49 or younger, $32,500 if you're age 50 or older.

The non-Roth after-tax contribution option to a 401(k)-type employer-sponsored plan, like its non-deductible traditional IRA counterpart explained above, has limited utility standing alone. As the name implies, there is no deduction on the contribution. The only tax benefit is tax deferment on the earnings.

That's why employees don't even want to think about making this type of contribution unless they're planning to contribute beyond the contribution limit.

Contributions that count against these limits can be made as a traditional contribution, where you enjoy a tax deduction and tax deferment on the contribution. This is superior to the non-Roth after-tax option, as there is deferment on both earnings and the contribution.

Since 2006, employers are also allowed to offer a Roth contribution option (not all do). This option, if offered, also counts toward the plan limits. It does not afford a tax deduction like the traditional option, but earnings accrue tax-free rather than tax deferred. This is superior to the non-Roth after-tax option too in that earnings accrue tax-free rather than tax deferred.

Once those limits are met, those select employees who are offered this non-Roth after-tax option in their 401(k)-type plan can choose to save in this manner in addition to their "regular" contributions.

As mentioned, this option is inferior to a Roth because your earnings are accruing tax deferred, not tax-free. That's why you'll want to initiate a conversion of those contributions (and any accumulated earnings) to a Roth IRA.

Convert to a Roth IRA

Some 401(k)-type plans allow conversions of these non-Roth after-tax contributions and associated earnings to a Roth IRA even if you're not yet age 59 1/2. Check with your plan to see if this option is available.

Not so with your traditional and/or Roth contributions that count toward the contribution maximums: they're locked up until you separate from service (or reach age 59 1/2 if your employer allows in-service withdrawals from the plan).

The beauty of 401(k)-type plan switcheroo is you can contribute well beyond the contribution limits allowed in these plans. I've seen some plans that allow contributions of this type all the way up to the yearly maximum allowed for defined contribution plans, which is $72,000 in 2026.

For example, say you are a 38-year-old super-saver higher wage earner with the above arrangements, and you've set your payroll deductions for the year to deduct the maximum $24,500. Let's further assume your contributions will generate a $6,000 company match, and your company offers a non-Roth after-tax 401(k) option.

You'd be able to save an extra $41,500 with the non-Roth after-tax contribution (72,000-24,500-6,000).

Some employers set a fixed contribution amount for their non-Roth after-tax option. Still others allow non-Roth after-tax 401(k) contributions to be "re-characterized" as Roth 401(k) contributions, saving you the necessity for a conversion.

Many employers who offer this third contribution option don't allow conversions to a Roth IRA or re-characterization options (unless you're separated from service, or your employer offers in-service withdrawals and you are age 59 ½ or older). Check your plan's rules to see if you are one of the lucky ones.

If your employer offers a 401(k)-type plan, be sure to check out all your savings options. If you can afford it, take full advantage of all the tax-advantaged options offered.

Author's Note: I first named this little trick the 'ole Roth IRA switcheroo over a decade ago when teaching high-tech employees this maneuver, but for some reason, the name never caught on. These days, it's most referred to as a *mega back-door Roth IRA.*

The Step Transaction Doctrine

There is no longer any need to fear the IRS's dreaded step transaction doctrine when performing any of the Switcheroos discussed above. I repeat, the IRS has backed off trying to enforce the step transaction doctrine as applied to either a Traditional IRA Switcheroo or an Employer Plan Switcheroo.

I make note of this because I have talked to many employees over the years who were reluctant to perform a Switcheroo because of possible trouble with the IRS.

In years past, taxpayers doing a Switcheroo potentially had to own up to the IRS as to "their intent."

The step transaction doctrine states that if several legal steps are taken by a taxpayer and they lead to a result that is not allowed, those several steps can be considered as one and disallowed if you were to get audited.

In the past, this could have been applicable to the Switcheroo where:

- A non-deductible IRA contribution was made to a traditional IRA (or a non-Roth after-tax contribution was made to your employer's retirement plan).

- Money was converted from a traditional IRA (or your employer's retirement plan) to a Roth IRA.

Both steps are allowed by the IRS; however, contributions to a Roth IRA are not allowed if you're over the income limits. The result, a contribution to a Roth IRA, was something you were prohibited from doing because you're over the limits.

The IRS applied three separate tests when evaluating transactions such as these in the past. Cutting to the chase, they tried to determine what your intent was at the time of your contribution.

At the time you made your non-deductible traditional IRA contribution, if your intent was to eventually convert that money to a Roth IRA, the transactions would fall under the step transaction doctrine and be disallowed.

For employer plan Switcheroos, it was even harder to prove your intent, especially if you converted all your after-tax contributions immediately after you made them, which is the most advantageous outcome from an earnings standpoint.

Hopefully, if you've had trepidation about performing a Switcheroo in the past, you feel better about things now as far as the IRS is concerned.

So, feel free to convert away your non-Roth after-tax contributions whenever you like, whether that be once a year, every quarter, or even after every contribution.

Remember, the sooner you get your non-Roth after tax contributions into a Roth IRA (or re-characterized within your 401(k)-type plan), the sooner you'll start enjoying tax-free earnings rather than tax-deferred earnings.

Conversions Versus Direct Roth IRA Contributions

How are these conversions different than if you were able to make a direct Roth IRA contribution? They are not immediately assessable tax and penalty free like direct Roth IRA contributions. You have to wait five years to pass for converted money to attain that status, and each year's conversion(s) has its own 5-year schedule.

That is, unless you're age 59 1/2 or older. Then those converted amounts are immediately available tax and penalty free. For the complete rundown on Roth IRA distribution rules check out the *IRS Ordering Rules: When Can I Start Tax-free Withdrawals?* chapter.

MAGI Limits Don't Really Matter

Even though it's a little sneaky, now just about everyone—regardless of the Roth IRA income limits—can enjoy tax-free earnings in a Roth IRA. It takes just one extra step, but that step could potentially save you tens of thousands of dollars in future tax liability.

Obviously, taking advantage of these Switcheroos can be very helpful if you're striving to reach financial independence sooner than later. Having access to contributions anytime and converted amounts five years after conversion is one way to get around the age 59 1/2 barrier.

The Switcheroos can be a blessing too if you're a bit behind on your retirement savings. They give you the ability to catch up in a hurry.

Roth Conversions and Rollovers

In the previous chapter, The 'Ole Roth IRA Switcheroo, we discussed one oddball-type of conversion that allows higher wage earners/super-savers to convert non-Roth after-tax money from a traditional IRA or employer retirement plan to a Roth IRA.

In this chapter we'll discuss more conventional conversions and rollovers.

Most likely you'll find you have several rollover and conversion options. Whichever you choose, maximizing your net after-tax return should be your ultimate goal.

Traditional IRA to a Roth IRA

A traditional IRA conversion to a Roth IRA is the easiest type to make. Both are private accounts. That means no employer rules get in the way.

Most if not all the money in your traditional IRA is probably of the pre-tax variety. It could have gotten there from a rollover from an old employer's plan, or maybe you made direct traditional IRA contributions when working for an employer who didn't offer a retirement plan.

Money you convert from a traditional IRA to a Roth IRA will be taxed at your marginal tax rate per ordinary income tax rates in the year of the conversion. If you're planning to convert a large amount and/or you have a high income, a lot of that money may get taxed at higher rates.

You don't have to convert all the money at once. Oftentimes, converting smaller amounts over time is a great strategy. This keeps you out of the higher tax brackets and reduces the amount of tax you'll pay.

You could also have *after-tax contributions in your traditional IRA*. If you do, things get a bit more complicated.

In the year you made a traditional IRA contribution, if you and/or your spouse made too much money (you were over the MAGI limits) and your employer or your spouse's employer offered a 401(k)-type plan, the deduction on your contribution would not have been allowed. Your contribution would be categorized as a non-deductible contribution.

That means when you make a qualified withdrawal of those funds, some of it would be taxable (the earnings), but the portion allotted to your principal contributions would be free of tax (you paid tax on it in the year of the contribution).

It's possible to have both these types of contributions and associated earnings in the same traditional IRA. Or the different types of contributions (pre-tax and post-tax) could be in separate traditional IRA accounts. As far as the IRS is concerned, it doesn't matter. They treat it as if it's all in one big pot for conversion purposes.

Beware the IRS's Pro Rata Rule

If you have both types, then you need to deal with the IRS's pro-rata rule. If you're not sure, check your account statements or old tax returns.

The pro-rata rule states you must convert a proportional amount of both deductible and non-deductible contributions from all your pre-tax accounts, including your traditional, SEP, and SIMPLE IRAs when doing a Roth IRA conversion.

This could put a damper on a popular strategy that I call the *'Ole Roth IRA Switcheroo* (page 41). For those whose income exceeds the income limits for a Roth IRA, a popular strategy is to first make a non-deductible traditional IRA contribution, for which there are no income limits, then at some point in the future convert those funds to a Roth IRA.

This strategy sounds sneaky but is perfectly legit; however, if you have both kinds of contributions (deductible and non-deductible), the pro-rata rule states that a pro-rata share of each must be converted – you can't choose which type you want to convert.

So, if you've made deductible traditional contributions in the past or rolled over a 401(k)-type plan to a traditional, SEP, or SIMPLE IRA, you may have to rethink your Switcheroo strategy.

401(k)-type plan to a Roth IRA

Before you convert or rollover money from your 401(k), 403(b), 401(a), 457 or other defined contribution plan to a Roth IRA, look at the details of your company's plan. Although most plans share many similar characteristics, your conversion, rollover, and withdrawal options are ultimately dictated by your employer.

Unless your company allows "in service withdrawals," which give still-employed workers the ability to withdraw money from their plans once they reach age 59 1/2, *separation from service* is a requirement to convert or rollover funds. That means you've either moved on, were let go, or retired.

Historically, employers allowed only traditional or pre-tax contributions to their plan. However, since 2006, employers have been given the option of amending their plans to allow a Roth contribution option, so you could have both types in your account.

Your former employer (or present employer if you're doing a qualified in-service withdrawal) may not have offered a Roth contribution option, but if they did, those Roth contributions and associated earnings can be rolled over to a Roth IRA free of tax or penalty. Those traditional or pre-tax contributions and earnings, however, are a different story.

Consider Your Tax Rate

Moving those traditional contributions and associated earnings from your former employer's retirement plan to a Roth IRA triggers tax on the entire amount converted. It will be taxed at your marginal tax rate per ordinary income tax rates in the year of the conversion. If you're planning to convert a large amount and/or you have a high income, a lot of that converted cash will get taxed at higher rates.

Crucial to your converting decisions will be the rate at which the converted funds will be taxed. That's why it's smart to plan your rollover/conversion around tax time.

This is especially important if your income varies from year to year. If you have a tax advisor, meet with them early to figure how much you want to convert. *The deadline for conversion is the end of the calendar year, not Tax Day like with contributions.*

Spreading your conversion out over several tax years could make sense. This strategy can keep that additional tax liability out of the higher tax brackets. Some employers' plans won't allow you to roll over funds multiple times: it's all or nothing. If that's the case, roll the money into a traditional IRA. Then you'll be able to convert those funds gradually over the years.

Also crucial to your decision is the amount of tax-free earnings you expect to generate from the time of the conversion until your projected withdrawal date. Generally, the longer the time horizon for investment, the more earnings you can expect to generate, and the greater benefit you'll derive from a conversion.

Given the fact that qualified Roth IRA earnings are free from all future federal tax, funds invested even at average rates of return will earn considerable future earnings if invested for fifteen or more years. Savvy investors with shorter time horizons may also generate considerable earnings.

Make sure you can afford to pay that extra tax out-of-pocket. Raiding your retirement plan to pay the taxes and suffering not only tax but a 10% penalty to boot rarely makes sense.

Check the details of your employer's plan, but the ability to convert to a Roth IRA is most likely just one of many options.

401(k)-type plan to Traditional IRA

You could do a traditional IRA rollover. If most or all your contributions to your employer's plan were pre-tax (traditional), this option is also affordable. No tax will be owed. If your 401(k) or other type plan contains both traditional and Roth contributions, you can rollover the traditional contributions and associated earnings into a traditional IRA and the Roth contributions and associated earnings into a Roth IRA, thus avoiding any penalty or tax.

401(k)-type plan to Next Employer's Plan

You can also rollover your funds tax and penalty free to your next employer's plan. Certainly, there is something to be said for consolidation. Plus, more than likely you'll be charged with 2 sets of administrative fees if you choose to keep both. Remember, one of the basic tenets of successful investing is keeping your expenses low.

Choose to Do Nothing

Another option is to *do nothing*. Usually, if your balance in your old employer's plan is greater than $5,000, most allow you to leave it there. You'll still have access to your investments and are able to manage things, but you can no longer make contributions to it.

Trustee to Trustee Transfer

No matter what you decide to do (sans doing nothing), make sure your conversion or rollover is done the right way. That means *not* withdrawing the money yourself and physically taking it to its new location. Contact the trustee of the old plan and the trustee of the new plan and let them handle the transfer.

That way you'll be assured of not being assessed a 10% early withdrawal penalty in addition to any tax.

Re-characterization

What if you contributed early in the year to your Roth IRA, not realizing your income was going to exceed the Roth IRA income limits?

The IRS, being the kind and gentle government bureaucracy that it is, offers remedies for this dilemma. The contribution, in addition to any associated earnings, can be moved back to a new or existing traditional IRA.

As of 2018 and the passage of the Tax Cuts and Jobs Act, *conversions* can no longer be re-characterized, just *contributions*.

This ends a popular strategy where money was converted to a Roth IRA during the calendar year. If those investments subsequently went up, the investor left it alone. If the investment went down before the deadline the investor re-characterizes, thus saving having to pay tax on "phantom income:" Income that no longer exists.

October 15th Deadline

That's October 15th (or the next business day) in the year *after* the calendar year for which the contribution was made.

For contributions made for calendar year 2026, you have until October 15, 2027, to re-do it. This deadline is the same as the due date of your 2026 tax return, plus extensions.

These options are available to you regardless of whether you requested an extension or have already filed your tax return. Obviously, if you already filed, an amended return would need to be filed to account for your extra tax savings.

Trustee to Trustee

As always, when I speak of "moving money" in the context of a conversion or rollover, I'm talking about a trustee-to-trustee transfer. That money "never touches your fingers." Your employer's 401(k)-type plan, a traditional IRA, and a Roth IRA are all required to be held by a trustee/custodian.

Their job is to oversee your account. Always have the respective trustee/custodians of the two accounts handle the conversion or rollover. That way you can be sure you won't be liable for unnecessary penalties and/or tax.

IRS Ordering Rules

The Roth IRA ordering rules allow tax and penalty-free withdrawals before age 59 1/2. This is a unique feature not found in many tax-advantaged accounts.

You may withdraw the value of your previous direct contributions at any time with no tax or penalty. You don't need a good reason, and you don't need to be age 59 1/2.

In fact, the IRS *requires* you to withdraw those direct contributions first. When you withdraw money from your Roth IRA(s), the IRS dictates in which order it's done.

If you have more than one Roth IRA, for accounting purposes the IRS looks at it as one big account, so it doesn't matter to which account(s) contributions were made or where money is withdrawn from.

This aggregate "account" could contain your past yearly contributions, any conversions and/or rollovers from a traditional IRA or employer-sponsored retirement account, and hopefully lots of earnings generated from your investments.

Contributions Come Out First

As discussed, you can withdraw an amount up to the value of your past direct contributions at any time, for any reason, completely free of tax and penalty. You don't have to wait 5 years or be age 59 1/2. It's that simple.

Example 1: Beth is 18 and has been accepted at several colleges. She worked after school during her senior year in high school and made $4,000. As a reward for her hard work, her mom gave her $2,000 to open and fund a Roth IRA in addition to Beth's $2,000 contribution. The value of the account is currently $4,500.

That autumn, Beth withdrew $4,000 tax and penalty-free from her Roth IRA to help pay for her tuition.

Example 2: Maurice, who is 58, has been contributing to his Roth IRA for years. Through shrewd investing, his $20,000 worth of direct contributions grew to $220,000. Maurice can only access his $20,000 of contributions tax and penalty-free right now. He'll have to wait for another 1 1/2 years (age 59 1/2) to access his $200,000 of earnings tax and penalty-free.

Converted Funds Come Second

If you converted funds to your Roth IRA in the past, the Roth IRA ordering rules state this money comes out next once the level of all past direct contributions has been reached.

Depending on what types of contributions you made and where that money was converted from, it was either "taxable" or "non-taxable" at the time of the conversion. Each type has its own set of rules and comes out in this order:

Taxable at the Time of Conversion

Monies converted in this category, which include conversions from 401(k)-type plans and traditional IRAs, must remain in your Roth IRA at least 5 years after the conversion to avoid the 10% early withdrawal penalty if you're under age 59 1/2 (unless one of the exceptions to the 10% early withdrawal penalty applies). Keep in mind if you converted funds in multiple calendar years, each year's conversion has its own 5-year clock. If you're age 59 1/2 or older, the converted funds can be taken out penalty-free at any time. In either case, no tax is owed upon withdrawal since you already paid it at the time of the conversion.

Non-Taxable at the Time of Conversion

Monies converted in this category, which include conversions from 401(k)-type plans (after-tax or Roth contributions only) and non-deductible traditional IRA contributions that were converted to a Roth IRA, can be withdrawn tax and penalty-free from your Roth IRA, but not until any "taxable at the time of conversion" monies have been tapped.

Earnings Come Out Last

After exhausting all your previous contributions and converted funds, earnings are the last to come out. To escape both the 10% early withdrawal penalty and tax, earnings must be considered "qualified," which means one or more of the following events have happened:

- You are 59 1/2 or older
- You are disabled
- You're dead (and the payment is made to your appointed beneficiary)
- You're withdrawing funds for a "first-time" Roth IRA home purchase

To escape tax as well as the penalty, withdrawals of earnings must also satisfy the *five-year rule*, which is *different* from the five-year rule for converted funds. This five-year rule simply states that counting from the date you made your first Roth contribution, 5 years must have passed.

This is measured from January 1 in the year in which the contribution was made, regardless of the year to which the contribution is attributed. (If you contributed for the previous year between January 1 and April 15, the starting date is January 1 in the year you contributed, not January 1 in the year for which the contribution was attributed.)

Exceptions to the 10% Early Withdrawal Penalty

Under the Roth IRA distributions rules, the 10% penalty will be avoided for non-qualified withdrawals under the following exceptions. Just because the penalty is avoided doesn't mean you won't pay tax–it may or may not be owed (see the IRS Ordering Rules above):

- Withdraw funds from your Roth IRA for college expenses
- Withdraw funds from your Roth IRA to pay for graduate school stipends and fellowships
- To pay for medical insurance premiums after losing your job
- To pay an IRS levy

- For unreimbursed medical expenses that exceed 10% of your adjusted gross income
- Qualified reservist, disaster recovery, or recovery assistance distribution
- To pay (up to $10,000) for childcare and adoption expenses up to 1 year after birth or adoption

Series of Substantial Equal Periodic Payments

Want to become financially independent before age 59 1/2? Here is another way to generate cash flow.

You can withdraw money from an IRA before age 59 1/2 without incurring a 10% penalty, and with a Roth IRA also avoid paying tax on withdrawals. A Series of Substantial Equal Periodic Payments (SEPP), often referred to as a 72(t) after the section of the Internal Revenue Code that defines it, gives you that ability. If you have an old 401(k)-type plan and are separated from service, you can do a 72(t) from that type of account as well.

SEPP payments can be set up on just one account or on multiple retirement accounts, so you could take SEPP withdrawals from a single Roth IRA and leave your other IRA(s) or dormant employer-sponsored account(s) alone. Once a payment schedule is established no other monies may be withdrawn, nor can any new contributions be made, until the SEPP payments are concluded.

SEPP payments involve using one of three IRS-allowable calculation methods (Amortization, Annuitization, or Required Minimum Distributions). A reasonable interest rate must be utilized to account for earnings that can't exceed 120% of the Federal Annual Mid-Term Rate, which is published monthly by the IRS.

These three methods rely on actuarial data, which establishes an amount that must be withdrawn yearly based on average lifespans. These payments must continue for at least five years or until you reach age 59 1/2, whichever is later.

Visit the IRS website *https://www.irs.gov/retirement-plans/retirement-plans-faqs-regarding-substantially-equal-periodic-payments* for more information regarding how to calculate payments, as well as frequently asked questions regarding setting up SEPP payments from your retirement plan.

A word of caution: Break any of the IRS rules, and they will slap a 10% early withdrawal penalty, as well as tax in some circumstances, on all withdrawals taken.

Try and Leave It Alone

To avoid having to understand these incredibly complex Roth IRA ordering rules and exceptions, as well as accumulating lots more tax-free earnings, *leave the money in your Roth IRA alone until at least 59 ½!*

Spousal Roth IRA: Double Your Tax Free Earnings

A spousal Roth IRA is the one exception to the Roth IRA contribution stipulation requiring earned income. A working spouse can effectively "give" income to their non-working partner, thus eliminating the requirement of earned income.

Tax Filing Requirements

Couples need to file their taxes as married filing jointly, not married filing separately, to qualify. In addition, the working spouse's earned income for the year must meet or exceed the total amount of contributions to all IRAs by the couple for that year.

Types of Contributions

A spousal IRA can consist of traditional contributions, Roth contributions (if you're under the limits), or both. This allows couples with one income source to save in up to four different accounts, diversifying how they save for retirement.

As an example, a married couple in their 40s has one working spouse whose employer does not offer a retirement plan, and they are under the income limits for making a Roth IRA contribution. They could contribute up to $15,000 in 2026: $7,500 in a traditional IRA and/or Roth IRA for the working spouse, and $7,500 in the spousal IRA (traditional, Roth, or a combination).

Our couple could contribute up to $17,200 if they were both age 50 or older.

Spousal Roth IRA and other Retirement Plans

If the working spouse's employer offers a retirement plan and the working spouse is a participant, the couple could save up to the limits of the retirement plan plus their IRAs, depending on income.

Spousal Roth IRA Switcheroo

What type of contribution(s) the couple would be allowed to make to their IRAs is determined by their Modified Adjusted Gross Income and the IRS income limits for the year. If you make too much money and are over the Roth IRA income limits, you might have to perform what I like to call the Ole Roth IRA Switcheroo.

Back to Work

If the non-working spouse decides to go back to work, he or she won't have to open another Roth

IRA to continue making Roth contributions (although they could if they wanted to). Contributions can be made directly to the same account containing the spousal contributions, and all money withdrawn will be 100% tax-free (assuming qualified withdrawals are made).

In fact, there really is no such thing as a "spousal Roth IRA"; it's just a Roth IRA. Whether you contribute money under the spousal Roth IRA rules or have income to support your own contribution is inconsequential. These two types of contributions—and their associated tax-free earnings—are treated the same and can be commingled.

A spousal Roth IRA contribution is especially helpful when a parent takes time off work to care for children. Contributions do not have to be curtailed. Remember, dollars you put in your Roth IRA early on will have a bigger bang for the buck than the ones invested later, so it's best to continue to contribute, even if it's just a few dollars.

Multiple Spousal Roth IRAs

You can have one or more spousal Roth IRAs going at the same time. The IRS doesn't care how many you have, as long as you make qualified contributions and don't go over the contribution limit for the year.

One reason you may want to have more than one account is to save on expenses. For instance, say both certificates of deposit and individual stocks are part of your Roth IRA investment plan. A local credit union may be your lowest cost choice for the Roth IRA cd investment, while a discount broker would be more affordable for buying and selling stocks.

Opening and Investing

It's easy to open a spousal Roth IRA, or any "type" of Roth IRA for that matter. Pretty much any financial institution that offers investments will offer a Roth. You'll then have access to most if not all the financial products that company offers.

The Spousal Roth IRA Advantage

Double the amount you save into IRAs by using the spousal Roth IRA option. Assuming you plan on staying married, treat you and your spouse's retirement plans as one big pot with just one investment plan, and try and maximize your contributions into that pot every year.

Minor Roth IRA and Savers Credit

A minor Roth IRA may be the single best thing (financially speaking) you can do for your kids. Combining a child's long time horizon for investment and low tax bracket makes it one of the most powerful saving tools available.

No Age Limit

There is no age limit for opening and investing in a Roth IRA. Earned income is the only requirement, but the earned income must be legit. Paying your kid to mow the lawn doesn't qualify. It must be actual earned income that is subject to income taxes.

Years ago, my own teenager had income for the first time from a job during high school, making her eligible to open a Roth IRA. I encouraged her to invest by sweetening the pot: I told her I'd match whatever she contributed. She contributed $500, so I kicked in an extra $500.

Most folks are unaware that a $1,000 contribution can be taken out by the owner of the Roth IRA *at any time, for any reason, without tax or penalty.* You don't have to be age 59 1/2, wait 5 years, or even have a good reason. Since she is now 18+ and the custodial designation has been removed, she is free to do so.

I've got a feeling she's going to leave it alone. She's understands the power of compounding and tax-free earnings. When I say earning tax-free earnings on your tax-free earnings, she knows what I'm talking about!

Seriously, kids that age benefit most from Roth IRA contributions. First, most are in very low tax brackets. My daughter, in fact, didn't owe any tax that year. It just made sense for her to get that tax liability, in this case zero dollars, "over with" in the year of the contribution.

Savers Credit 2026

The saver's credit of up to $2,000 ($4,000 if married filing jointly) applies to contributions made to IRAs, 401(k)-type plans, as well as other types of retirement accounts, but you must meet the following income requirements:

Savers Credit 2026			
tax credit rate	married filing jointly	head of household	*all others
50% of contribution	AGI not more than $48,500	AGI not more than $36,375	AGI not more than $24,250
20% of contribution	$48,501-$52,500	$36,376-$39,375	$24,251-$26,250
10% of contribution	$52,501-$80,500	$39,376-$60,375	$26,251-$40,250
No credit	over $80,500	over $60,375	over $40,250
*single, married filing separately, or qualifying widow			

What's Your AGI?

Your AGI or adjusted gross income is your gross income minus "adjustments to income" on schedule 1040 or schedule 1040a. Adjustments to income are available to all taxpayers, regardless of whether you itemize or take the standard deduction.

Following are the more popular adjustments to income:

- traditional IRA contributions
- student loan interest
- tuition and fees
- health savings account contribution
- early withdrawal penalty
- self-employment taxes and health insurance (if self-employed)

Any Retirement Contribution Will Do

It doesn't matter whether you contribute to a Roth IRA, traditional IRA, or SEP IRA, or if you contribute to your employer's 401(k), 403(b), 457, 401(a), or another qualified plan. You're still eligible for the tax credit if you're under the AGI limits.

Custodial Account Required

Aspiring Roth IRA savers under the age of majority—age 18 in most states—cannot legally own assets until they reach the age of majority, but a simple custodial Roth IRA does the trick in the interim.

A custodial account is no big deal. They are inexpensive (usually free), and readily available, and the custodial designation is easily removed once the child reaches the age of majority. It simply involves a parent (or other adult) signing on to take responsibility for the account until the minor is of legal age.

A Real Life Example

What my daughter really has going for her is a long-time horizon for investment—let's say 45 years. Figuring a 7% return on her money (compounded monthly) that $1,000 will turn into around $23,000. That $22,000 of earnings will be completely free from taxes when she reaches age 59 1/2. The $1,000 contribution has already been subject to tax, so that can be withdrawn tax-free as well.

Had she instead made a traditional IRA contribution, both principal ($1,000) and earnings ($22,000) would be fully taxable at whatever federal, state, and local ordinary income tax rates apply in the second half of the twenty-first century. If I had to guess, I'd say they're going to be higher than they are now.

Beware of High Investment Thresholds

More than likely your kids are going to start off investing small amounts. That's perfectly OK. As the previous example illustrates, money contributed early on has quite a big bang for the buck. Even a few dollars will go a long way.

You may, however, run into some difficulty finding a financial institution that will accept such small amounts, especially initially. I had to shop around when looking for where to open my daughter's Roth IRA account (all she had was $1,000).

The trick is finding high-performing mutual funds with low costs that don't have high initial investment thresholds. I ended up opening her account at T. Rowe Price®. Their fees are low and their funds have good performance records, and setting up the custodial designation was a snap. Unfortunately, they've since raised the minimum investment thresholds on most of their accounts. I've since had my daughter transfer her account to Vanguard®.

Vanguard® (and others) offer low-cost Exchange Traded Funds that have no minimum investment thresholds. Your minimum is simply the cost of a single share. And since Vanguard® doesn't charge brokerage fees, a diversified portfolio can be created with very little cash.

Kids and Money

Besides helping to jump-start their retirement savings, a Roth IRA has another advantage—teaching your kids financial literacy. Why simple skills like reconciling an account, basic investing, and the time value of money are not taught in our secondary schools—or our colleges for that matter—is beyond me.

That leaves the education up to you, the parent. Establishing a Roth IRA for them as early as possible will help you teach them those much-needed life skills. Plus, when tax-free earnings start piling up, kids take notice.

The Gift That Keeps on Giving

There is no finer gift to give your kids than those of wealth and financial literacy. Help them open up and manage a Roth IRA as soon as they have earned income. They'll love you for it more and more as time goes by!

Designating Your Roth Beneficiary

Properly filling out your beneficiary statement(s) is the first step in creating a powerful wealth building tool for the next generation. Besides saving for retirement, Roth investments have unique qualities that can be used to help pass money on to the next generation.

Roth investments in 401(k)-type plans currently are subject to required minimum distributions (see below) even though no tax liability is due on withdrawals. This is easily avoided once you separate from service from your employer (you move on to another job or retire) by rolling all Roth contributions and associated earnings tax and penalty-free into a Roth IRA.

Unlike most retirement accounts, Roth IRAs are not subject to required minimum distributions (RMDs). RMDs kick in for those reaching age 73 in 2023. The bottom line is your pre-tax retirement accounts may be empty by the time you reach the latter years of your retirement.

Save Your Roth IRA Till Last

Tap other retirement accounts first and save your Roth IRA until last. Thanks to no RMDs, that gives you a longer time horizon for investment, allowing you more time to accumulate tax-free cash.

What if you don't make it to the latter years of your retirement? Let's say you get run over by a bus. (I tried to make it as painless as possible for you.) Your loved ones, those named Roth IRA beneficiaries, get the tax-free cash rather the taxable variety.

Rules and procedures must be followed to insure all money is tax-free. Let me take you, step by step, from beginning to end. The information provided will aid both the account holder and the beneficiary.

The All Important Beneficiary Statement

A properly completed Roth IRA beneficiary statement is all that's needed to insure a hassle-free exchange at the time of the account holder's death. It is a legitimate will substitute, meaning the money does not go through the probate process.

The names you write on the Roth IRA beneficiary statement supersede any instructions in your will that may be contrary. Absent any extenuating circumstances, if you have Sally as your primary Roth IRA beneficiary and you say that Billy gets the Roth in your will, Sally ends up with the proceeds.

If you want more than one beneficiary to inherit your Roth IRA, put all of them on the primary beneficiary line with percentages of inheritance, if appropriate. If Sally is on the primary beneficiary line and Billy is on the secondary beneficiary line, Sally gets the money once again. Only if Sally pre-deceased the account holder would Billy inherit the Roth IRA.

Fill out both the primary and secondary beneficiary sections. Catastrophes are rare but do occur. Familiarize yourself with the Latin terms Per Stirpes and Per Capita, especially if children are named beneficiaries.

"Estate planning speak" can be confusing, but many financial institutions insist on using it. It's best to consult an attorney licensed in your state of residence if there is any doubt.

Spouse as Beneficiary

A spouse has many options when he or she is named as the Roth IRA beneficiary:

- Leave the Roth IRA as is and take payments via the deceased spouse's schedule
- Roll it into their own Roth IRA tax and penalty-free

Regardless of which option is chosen, the surviving spouse would have immediate tax-free access to the principal, just as the deceased spouse would have during their lifetime. At what point the earnings could be withdrawn tax-free would be determined by the respective ages of the spouses and the length of time the Roth IRA had been open.

Non-Spouse as Beneficiary

In most states, you can't name a non-spouse as your beneficiary if you are married unless the spouse gives up their rights. This is usually done through an addendum which may require the spouse's notarized signature.

A non-spouse beneficiary should set up a separate inherited Roth IRA to receive the funds, which will include the decedent's name in the title. The beneficiary has immediate access to the principal contributions of the decedent, as well as earnings if the account was established by the decedent more than five years before.

If a non-spouse beneficiary wishes to delay withdrawals, they can do so for ten years. After ten years (starting with the year after the decedents death), all money must be distributed to the beneficiary thanks to the Secure Act, which took effect on January 1, 2020. This effectively ended the "stretch IRA" for most, which allows named beneficiaries to make distributions over their lifetime, with the following exceptions in regard to the beneficiary:

- Is no more than 10 years younger than decedent
- Is disabled or chronically ill
- Is a minor (only until minor reaches the age of majority)

IRAs containing certain existing commercial annuities are also exempt from the 10-year distribution rule.

These rules apply to both Roth and traditional IRAs, but of course are more apropos to traditional IRAs, as traditional IRA beneficiaries have more incentive to delay withdrawals (to delay paying tax owed on those withdrawals).

Tax-free Cash for Your Beneficiaries

Besides being a powerful retirement planning tool, a Roth IRA can also help you meet many estate planning objectives. Extended tax-free earnings and no required minimum distributions are unique to a Roth IRA, so be sure to take full advantage.

Make sure that Roth IRA beneficiary statement is properly filled out, and review it periodically along with your other important estate planning documents.

Important: Before filling out important legal documents like a Roth IRA beneficiary statement or titling assets like an inherited Roth IRA, consult an attorney licensed in your state of residence.

Self-Directed Roth IRAs

The IRS rules governing self-directed Roth IRAs aren't so much complex as vague. Life insurance and collectibles are specifically disallowed, as are specific types of transactions, but beyond that there is not much guidance.

This has led to some creative Roth IRA investment solutions by enterprising IRA custodians/trustees over the years. The problem is many have later been disallowed by the IRS. That triggers a liquidation and subsequent distribution as of the first year of the investment, and all tax and early withdrawal penalties apply.

That's why you must be careful if you pursue a self-directed Roth IRA. Choose one that has a track record with the IRS, and be wary of risky, non-diversified investments that may not be appropriate for your hard-earned retirement dollars.

There are lots of sharks in the self-directed IRA waters. Many fraudulent investment schemes involve self-directed IRAs. Before investing in one, you must read this short article published by the Securities and Exchange Commission: *Investor Alert: Self-Directed IRAs and the Risk of Fraud*. Find it at: *https://www.investor.gov/additional-resources/news-alerts/alerts-bulletins/investor-alert-self-directed-iras-risk-fraud.*

You can set up a self-directed *traditional* IRA as well—the same rules apply. The only difference is qualified distributions from a self-directed traditional IRA are taxable while qualified distributions from a self-directed Roth IRA are tax-free.

Roth IRA LLC

A Roth IRA LLC is not an investment. It's a popular ownership structure where a limited liability company (LLC) is formed. The LLC is owned by the self-directed IRA, and the IRA is cared for by the custodian, who you'll need to hire to look after things per IRS rules.

Besides limiting the amount of your liability, an LLC gives you the ability to invest in non-conventional investments which most Roth IRA custodians don't offer. You can direct your custodian to purchase real estate, metals, make private loans, invest in tax liens, or start a new business.

Real Estate

Roth IRA accounts can buy, manage, and sell real estate, but it's tricky to do. You're probably better off sticking with a REIT (Real Estate Investment Trust), limited partnership, or other form of indirect ownership if you want to diversify your Roth IRA with real estate.

Why? It has to do with running afoul of the IRS prohibited actions list. A disqualified person cannot be involved in the purchase and/or management of a property purchased by the Roth IRA, and that includes you and your family. That means collecting a rent check or sweeping the driveway could trigger severe negative financial penalties.

Many entities, like the LLC structure described above, attempt to circumvent these rules. Some have met with success: IRS rulings support the use of their particular structure. Others have been disallowed, along with penalties and tax being assessed retroactive to the first year of operation.

Caveats aside, investing in real estate through your Roth IRA can be done. Look for custodians/trustees that have proven real estate investment backgrounds, solid legal footing with the IRS, and *charge reasonable expenses* for their services.

Precious Metals

Wall Street offers plenty of ways to invest in gold, silver, platinum, palladium, and other precious metals. You can invest in companies that mine the mineral or buy precious metal mutual funds or exchange-traded funds, but most Roth IRA custodians don't give you the option of physically owning the mineral.

Self-directed Roth IRAs can give you that option. You need to select a Roth IRA custodian who is a dealer/broker in your metal and use an approved depository, if applicable. As with all self-directed Roth IRAs, there are plenty of rules and restrictions, so be sure to choose a custodian with a proven track record who knows the law.

Beware of unscrupulous custodians with high fees and shaky legal standing. There are plenty of "sharks" out there looking to take advantage in this area. Plus, oftentimes investing in commodities like precious metals makes the volatility of the stock market appear tame.

It may make sense to invest a *small portion* of your retirement dollars in precious metals, but rarely does it make sense to invest all or most of it.

Risk and Self-Directed Roth IRAs

That's the way it works with risk. Starting a new business, investing all your money in just one type of investment, buying a speculative piece of real estate, gambling on commodity prices, or making high interest loans to start-up businesses all can make you rich quickly, and through a self-directed Roth IRA these investments are possible.

Be sure to be realistic and look at the downside. Most start-up businesses fail, the commodity markets are highly unpredictable, and investing in just one thing leaves you susceptible to messing up your retirement savings big time.

Be smart with your money. Diversify your portfolio with both risky and not-so-risky investments. Include different types of investments in your investment plan, and always strive to keep your expenses low.

Using a Roth IRA for Other Financial Goals

Normally, I don't recommend combining financial goals. Saving for college, a home purchase, financial independence, and establishing an emergency reserve fund are four separate goals that should be saved for separately, and each should have its own unique investment plan to maximize returns and minimize risk. However, if money is tight, you can utilize a Roth IRA for all those purposes and more.

Remember, previous principal contributions to a Roth IRA can be accessed at any time, for any reason, without tax or penalty. According to the IRS ordering rules, it will be those funds that are withdrawn first. You can use those dollars for college, a first-time home purchase, retirement, medical expenses, a dream vacation, a new boat, a backyard makeover—*anything* your heart desires.

After those funds are exhausted, that's when the following exceptions to the 10% early withdrawal penalty kick in and become useful. You might owe *tax* on withdrawals, however. It depends on how the money arrived in your Roth IRA, whether through taxable conversions, non-taxable conversions, rollovers, or earnings from your investments.

Consult the IRS ordering rules chapter to determine any *tax liability* associated with your withdrawal.

Saving for College

There are provisions in IRAs that waive the 10% early withdrawal penalty for distributions to pay for qualified college expenses for you, your spouse, kids, or grandkids. That means a Roth IRA allows you to simultaneously save for both retirement and education in the same account(s).

Qualified college expenses include:

- Tuition
- Fees
- Books
- Room and board (if student enrolled at least half-time in a degree program)

Remember, previous direct contributions are deemed by the IRS to be accessed first, so those funds are available for college (or any other reason) penalty free. No tax will be owed on those withdrawals either: You paid tax on those amounts in the year of the contribution, so they're free of tax liability as well as the 10% early withdrawal penalty.

After those funds are exhausted, withdrawals will still avoid the 10% early withdrawal penalty if used to pay qualified college expenses, but might be subject to tax, depending on when and how they arrived in your Roth IRA (taxable conversions, non-taxable conversions, or earnings).

Also note distributions made from a Roth IRA — *regardless of whether they are taxable or non-taxable* — must be reported as income on the Free Application for Federal Student Aid (FAFSA). Potentially, this could hurt a student's chances of qualifying for grants and subsidized loans.

529 plans and Educational Savings Accounts are tax-advantaged savings plans designed specifically for saving for future educational expenses for you and your family. Earnings accrue tax-free provided funds are used for educational

purposes. Traditionally these are the vehicles of choice when saving for college.

However, given a Roth IRA's unique characteristics, it can be used to help pay for qualified college expenses for you and your family in a pinch. Make sure you're not being too generous and jeopardizing your own retirement and financial independence.

Buying a Home

The Roth IRA home purchase provision allows up to a $10,000 penalty-free withdrawal. You must be a "first time homebuyer" to qualify, which the IRS defines as a taxpayer who has not owned a home during the last two years.

This provision of the 1997 Taxpayer Relief Act also allows penalty-free withdrawals from a traditional IRA, but the Roth IRA home purchase rules are different. Deemed a "qualified" withdrawal by the IRS, all Roth IRA withdrawals for the purpose of a first time home acquisition avoid the 10% early withdrawal penalty as well as tax [if the taxpayer's (first) Roth IRA has been open for 5 years or more].

Once the distribution from your Roth IRA is taken for the purchase of that "first" home, the clock starts ticking. You must use it for "qualified acquisition costs" within 120 days of taking the distribution.

That's why it's best to *plan your distribution carefully and coordinate it with the escrow company* handling your purchase.

Qualified acquisition costs include down payments, building or re-building expense, escrow fees, appraisals, costs associated with obtaining financing, and recording fees—anything associated with the purchase, building, or re-building of a home.

Qualified acquisition costs **do not** include reducing the principal on your mortgage, furnishings, or a room addition.

If you have both a traditional IRA and a Roth IRA, the $10,000 limit applies to both combined, not each, and you can only use the provision once in your lifetime. Married couples maintaining separate IRAs have a $20,000 limit ($10,000 each from the couple's respective IRAs).

The IRS ordering rules say any principal contributions previously made directly to your Roth IRA come out first. So, if you made direct Roth IRA contributions of say, $60,000 over the years, you could take out that entire amount tax and penalty free for the purchase of a home... or a new car... or a European vacation... or any other reason you can think of...

Assuming no previous withdrawals had been made, you may not need to use the Roth IRA home purchase provision to withdraw money for the purchase of your principal residence if your previously untapped contributions total $10,000 or more. Principal contributions can be taken out for any reason, at any time, with no tax or penalty, and the IRS ordering rules deem those contributions are "the first to come out."

Once those direct contributions are exhausted, it gets a bit more complicated.

Buying a Home Example

Ali is 32 years old, opened her Roth IRA six years ago, and wants to withdraw $10,000 from her Roth IRA to help with the down payment on her soon-to-be new home. She's made no previous withdrawals from IRAs. Her current Roth IRA account balance is $15,000 and consists of the following:

Ali's Roth IRA Contributions	$8,000
Funds converted from her traditional IRA 3 years ago	$1,500
Earnings	$5,500
Total:	**$15,000**

First out is the $8,000 of principal, which is never subject to any tax or penalty under any circumstances.

Next out is the $1,500 converted amount from her traditional IRA. Normally, since Ali is not yet 59 1/2 and five years have not yet passed since the conversion, this amount would be subject to a 10% penalty, but the penalty is waived because the Roth IRA home purchase provision makes it a qualified withdrawal. It's not taxable either—Ali paid the tax on it when she converted it three years ago.

Last out is $500 worth of earnings. Normally, this amount would be subject to both tax and penalty, but the penalty and tax are both waived because the Roth IRA home purchase provision deems it a qualified withdrawal.

Back-up Emergency Reserve Fund

If you don't already have an emergency reserve fund, think seriously about socking away three to twelve months of expenses into a savings or money market account for "unforeseen" expenses. Having an emergency reserve fund helps you sleep a little better at night.

Have you been conscientiously making contributions over the years to your Roth IRA? If so, I think it's perfectly acceptable to assign a portion of your emergency reserve fund to your Roth IRA, but only after you've got a big chunk of contributions stashed away.

Over the years, I've noticed I never once had to access the latter half of my emergency reserve fund (knock on wood). I've had to tap the first half of it plenty of times, for everything from a blown gasket in my truck to a big medical bill for a family member.

As my wife and I have gotten older and we've continued to contribute to our Roth IRAs, I have backed off on the amount we keep in our emergency reserve fund.

Knowing those previous Roth IRA contributions are totally accessible without tax or penalty if needed, I'm gambling that our good luck holds. If it doesn't and we need cash above and beyond what we have in our now smaller emergency reserve fund, those contributions invested in our Roth IRAs are available, even though neither one of us have turned age 59 1/2 yet.

Say you normally keep $30,000 in a money market account as your emergency reserve, and you've made $80,000 of contributions to your Roth IRA over the years. You could reduce your emergency reserve fund to $20,000 or $15,000, knowing you can access those past contributions if that need ever arises without messing up your retirement savings too much.

Chances are you won't have to, but you're still covered if disaster strikes.

Roth Investments and Your Financial Plan

Whether you're a seasoned investor, novice, or somewhere in between, an investment plan is a must-have for all your financial goals. It doesn't need to be complicated, but if you don't have one you won't be as successful an investor as you could be.

Your investment plan for financial independence might be just one mutual fund in a single Roth IRA at this point if you're just starting out. Or, you may have several Roth IRAs, along with 401(k)-type plans from previous employers.

Whether you're at one of those extremes or somewhere in between, make sure the following risk management strategies are part of your plan. Applying these strategies isn't rocket science. Once you've grasped them, it just doesn't make sense for you to pay someone big bucks to apply them for you.

Essential Risk Management Strategies

What is your time horizon for investment? This is the first question you should ask yourself before formulating any plan.

Generally speaking, the longer your time horizon for investment, the riskier your portfolio should be. Conversely, the shorter the time horizon the more conservative.

Even ultra-conservative investors with long-term horizons need at least some risk in their portfolios to keep up with inflation. You may not be literally losing money with an ultra-conservative investment over the long term, but you will be figuratively as the buying power of that money is diminished.

A Diversified Portfolio

If you have a 15-year-plus time horizon, a good chunk of your investment plan dollars should be invested in a *diversified portfolio of stocks*. Stocks tend to be great long-term investments but can be wildly unpredictable in the short term.

That's why when investing for the shorter term (4 years or less), less volatile bonds should be used instead of stock. Bonds are fixed income, non-equity investments where rates of return are lower, but your principal is less at risk than when investing in stocks.

Diversification means not only mixing in both stocks and bonds but diversifying on both the stock and the bond side.

On the stock side, you can diversify by acquiring different size companies (small cap, mid cap and large cap), by investing style (income and growth), as well as mixing in an international element.

On the bond side, diversify by maturity length (short, intermediate, and long) and amount of business risk (conservative, moderate, and aggressive).

A Dynamic Stock to Bond Ratio

Besides diversifying both the stock and bond sides of your portfolio, consider coming up with what I like to call a *dynamic stock to bond ratio*. As your time horizon for investment begins to change, so should your stock to bond ratio.

Be heavy in stocks when you have a lengthy horizon but shift assets over to safer bonds as that time horizon gets shorter. In other words, a dynamic stock to bond ratio means shifting from a more aggressive portfolio to a more conservative portfolio as your time horizon shrinks.

Once you reach your withdrawal date, the money you plan to tap in the very near future (1-2 years) should be devoid of any risk (in a money market or insured savings account).

Rebalancing and Reassessing

Make these changing stock and bond ratios part of your investment plan, which means deciding now what your stock to bond ratio is going to be at present, next year, and if appropriate 5, 10, 15, and 20+ years hence.

Don't make it complicated. Pull out your investment plan *once a year* on *the same date* and make any adjustments per the plan. For example, your plan may call for you to change from this year's 70% stock 30% bond ratio to next year's 68% stock 32% ratio.

You never want your stock to bond ratio to be riskier next year than the year before. It should either stay the same or be slightly more conservative (i.e. more bonds) than the year before.

At the same time you are reassessing your investment plan, make sure you *rebalance* it too.

Rebalancing helps iron out some of that volatility inherent in the stock market. If stocks have gone up the past year, rebalancing involves banking some of your "winnings" by shifting money from stocks to safer bonds. If stocks performed poorly, money shifts back from bonds to stocks in anticipation of a stock upturn.

Simply put, rebalancing gets you back to the level of risk dictated by your investment plan. If you started out 70-30 stocks to bonds and one year later after a good year for stocks you're now at 80-20, rebalancing will get you back to where you want to be (70-30). Same if it's a bad year for stocks. That 70-30 stock to bond ratio now may be 60-40. Rebalance it back to 70-30 and leave your plan alone for another year.

How Comfortable Are You with Risk?

Everyone has different tolerances for risk. That's why it's smart to incorporate the risk management strategies discussed above (dynamic stock to bond ratio, diversification, and rebalancing and reassessing) into your investment plan. These risk management strategies help smooth out those inherent risks as you decrease the volatility of your portfolio.

Still, especially if you have a longer time horizon for investment, your portfolio will be volatile, wildly volatile at times, since a good deal of money is invested in stocks. That's why stock and bonds ratios can vary greatly, even for investors with similar time horizons.

Investors that can accept these ups and downs and realize you're *not* going to make money every single year in the stock market have had better luck sticking to their investment plans when the going gets tough. That's not easy to do, especially in the face of a big financial debacle like 2008, but your success as an investor depends on it.

Look to 2020 for Guidance

Look at the initial Covid 19 stock market crash in late March of 2020 for perspective. Sans a crystal ball that would have told you when the highs and lows of the stock market would occur (which no one had), your best move back then would have been to stick to your investment plan.

That meant stomaching 30% plus losses in the stock market, depending on the aggressiveness of your plan. It also meant investing new money, per your Roth contribution schedule dictated by your investment plan, into that volatile and unsettled stock market.

To date, you've regained all your losses and then some. Just as importantly, those new contributions you made when stocks were down in the dumps yielded you most excellent gains by buying low and selling high.

You probably already have a good idea about your tolerance for risk. Adjust your stock to bond ratio accordingly so you'll stick to your plan during that next stock market debacle. If your withdrawal date happens to coincide with one of those downturns, your goal comes to fruition anyway. Your always-getting-more-conservative dynamic stock to bond ratio will save you, and you can afford to leave your now smaller stock percentage alone until it goes back up.

Taking this long-term outlook on the stock market and incorporating these risk management strategies is the way to go in my opinion. You're not going to get rich quick, but you're not going to lose most or all your money either.

Applying those risk management strategies yourself and utilizing low-cost investments can save you big bucks on fees. Investing those saved commissions and fees makes a big positive difference over time.

Choose Your Level of Involvement

If you're not willing to spend the small amount of time it takes to manage and monitor your investments, you're better off getting some help. This help may be in the form of a balanced or target maturity mutual fund or from a financial advisor or stockbroker. Either way, you're going to pay for it.

Target Retirement Funds

Target retirement fund managers do in fact incorporate all three risk management strategies into your plan, and they manage your money for you per the assumed time horizon for investment. That's how target retirement plans work: You put all your money in the target fund with the date (2025, 2030, 2035, 2040, 2045, etc.) closest to your own projected date of starting withdrawals, and the manager of the fund automatically incorporates all three strategies for you.

You Pay for Those Extra Services

However, don't think those extra services—a dynamic stock to bond ratio, diversification, and reassessing and rebalancing—are done for free. They're not. Extra fees for those services are reflected in the expense ratio of those target funds.

You can save on fees by doing it yourself. If you're offered a target retirement option in your employer's plan or IRA, try this experiment.

Construct your own diversified portfolio with individual stock and bond mutual funds using the same investing style as the target retirement fund, then compute the average expense ratio of that portfolio. (Be sure to account for the varying percentages of the mutual funds that make up the mix.) More than likely the result will be less than the target fund's expense ratio.

These higher fees really add up over the years. Plus, by constructing your own investment plan, you'll have a bigger say in what you're investing in rather than relying strictly on the target fund manager.

Your other option is to hire someone to do it for you. Very few investment professionals, when you consider those extra brokerage charges and fees, justify that extra expense. In fact, many times it's much worse because there is also a conflict of interest: The success of their own financial goals is dependent on the fees they charge you. Remember, no one cares more about your money than you do.

One Investment Plan

Most investors approaching financial independence have accumulated many *accounts* over the years from multiple employers and pursuits. What I'm advocating is a single *investment plan* for each financial goal, despite the number of accounts.

Oftentimes it's advantageous to maintain multiple accounts: For instance, if you like picking individual securities, you could trade stocks through a Roth IRA at a discount broker yet hold other assets elsewhere.

You're smart if you have just one investment plan for all those accounts. Treat them as one. If you're married (and plan to stay that way), add your spouse's retirement assets to the pot. Don't fret over each account separately; treat them all as one big account and invest accordingly.

The money in these multiple accounts have the same time horizon for investment and are for the same purpose, so it's much easier to have just one investment plan rather than many separate investment plans for each account.

You'll need a customized spread sheet, portfolio management software, financial app, or other such information-consolidating device to put the data from those various accounts all in one place.

If you have a small amount of money in one of those accounts, it could be next to impossible to diversify that one account properly because of limited funds and minimum investment thresholds. However, by artificially "merging it" with your other accounts, creating proper asset allocation and diversity is much easier.

For example, maybe your spouse's Roth IRA contains only stock mutual funds invested in small company domestic stock. That's *not* a diversified investment plan. But when you combine it with your other investments in other accounts, which consist of large company domestic stock, some international stock investments, plus a diversified bond element, it fits perfectly.

Choosing Your Own Best Roth

Thank you for reading my book on building tax-free wealth with Roth IRAs and 401(k)-type plans, the second book in my *Becoming Financially Independent* book series. Hopefully, you've got a better idea of how your Roth(s) fit into your investment plans for your longer-term goals like financial independence and retirement.

I urge you to continue learning. Contributing to Roth accounts helps, but so does having an exceptional investment strategy.

Next up in my series is *DIY Stock and Securities Investing: Investment Strategies for Building Wealth and Attaining Financial Independence*. Even though I'm a licensed Certified Financial Planner®, I don't want to manage your money. I want to teach you how to do it.

Whether you're managing an already diverse portfolio or just getting started, *DIY Stock and Securities Investing* will help you minimize risk and maximize returns, while keeping your investment expenses to a bare minimum. It explains my risk management strategies, introduces my 5 tenets of successful stock investing, and much more.

Keep the 250-page paperback version and its detailed Table of Contents handy to answer future investing questions.

I wish you the best of luck. Be prosperous and safe.

###

About Keith Dorney

Keith Dorney was a 2-time All-American offensive tackle at Penn State University from 1975-78. He also earned Academic All-American honors and was elected to the College Football Hall of Fame in 2005.

The 10th pick in the 1st round of the 1979 NFL draft, he was chosen by the Detroit Lions where he played his entire career. Dorney received numerous honors as a professional, including Pro Bowl, All-Pro, and team MVP honors, and served as team captain from 1983-1987.

Post-football, Dorney turned to writing and teaching. A memoir, *Black and Honolulu Blue* (September 2003–Triumph Books) was his first book.

While earning his MA in Teaching (University of San Francisco), Dorney's resume included teaching Juvenile Hall-sanctioned programs and high school English.

More recently, Dorney turned to corporate training, informing employees of Google®, Microsoft®, Cisco Systems®, Roche®, and other Fortune 500 companies how to maximize employee benefits and reach financial independence sooner.

A Certified Financial Planner® since 2010, Dorney now writes and teaches full-time from his farm south of Sebastopol, California, where he and his wife Katherine raised their two kids and still reside.

When not writing or teaching, he enjoys hanging out in the garden and spending time with family and friends.

Detailed Table of Contents